This book is
ultimately dedicated
to our baby girl
Amara Celestine J. Basa,
sons
Niel Michael J. Basa
and
Jasper Miguel J. Basa.

INTRODUCTION

Have fun with Alphabets is an introduction to Alphabets by using images. Toddlers first recognize letters by its sound. Recognizing the images will help them identify, differentiate and pronounce the 28 Filipino alphabets.

This book will also help kids write alphabet for the first time by tracing down the letters.

THE FILIPINO ALPHABET

Aa Bb Cc Dd Ee

Ff Gg Hh Ii Jj Kk

Ll Mm Nn NGng

Ññ Oo Pp Qq Rr

Ss Tt Uu Vv Ww

Xx Yy Zz

Learn to write

Aa

A

A

a

a

An Airplane

Aa

Avocado

apple

Ant

angel

Axe

acorn

Learn to write

Bb

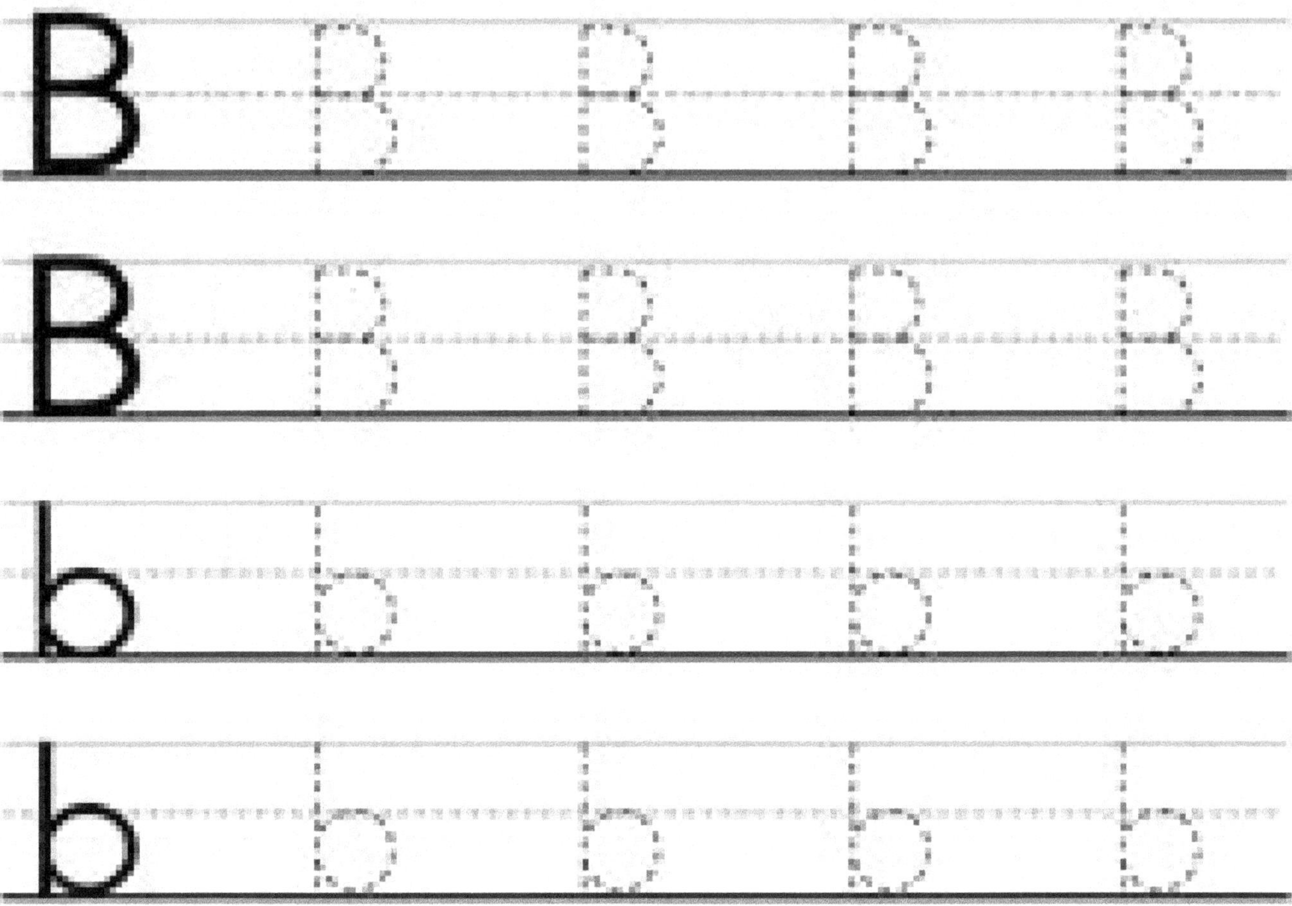

Blue Bell

Bb

Ball

bus

Boots

banana

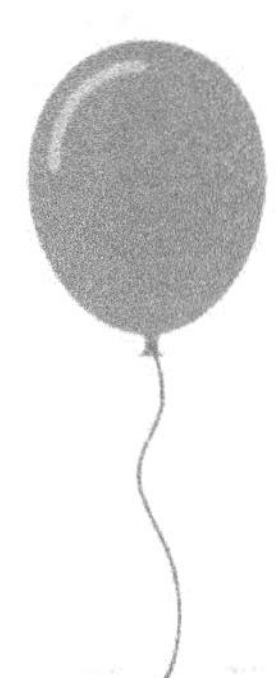

Baloon

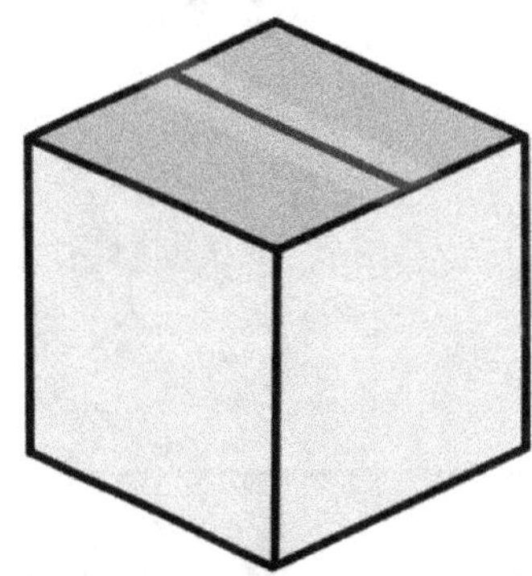

box

Learn to write

Cc

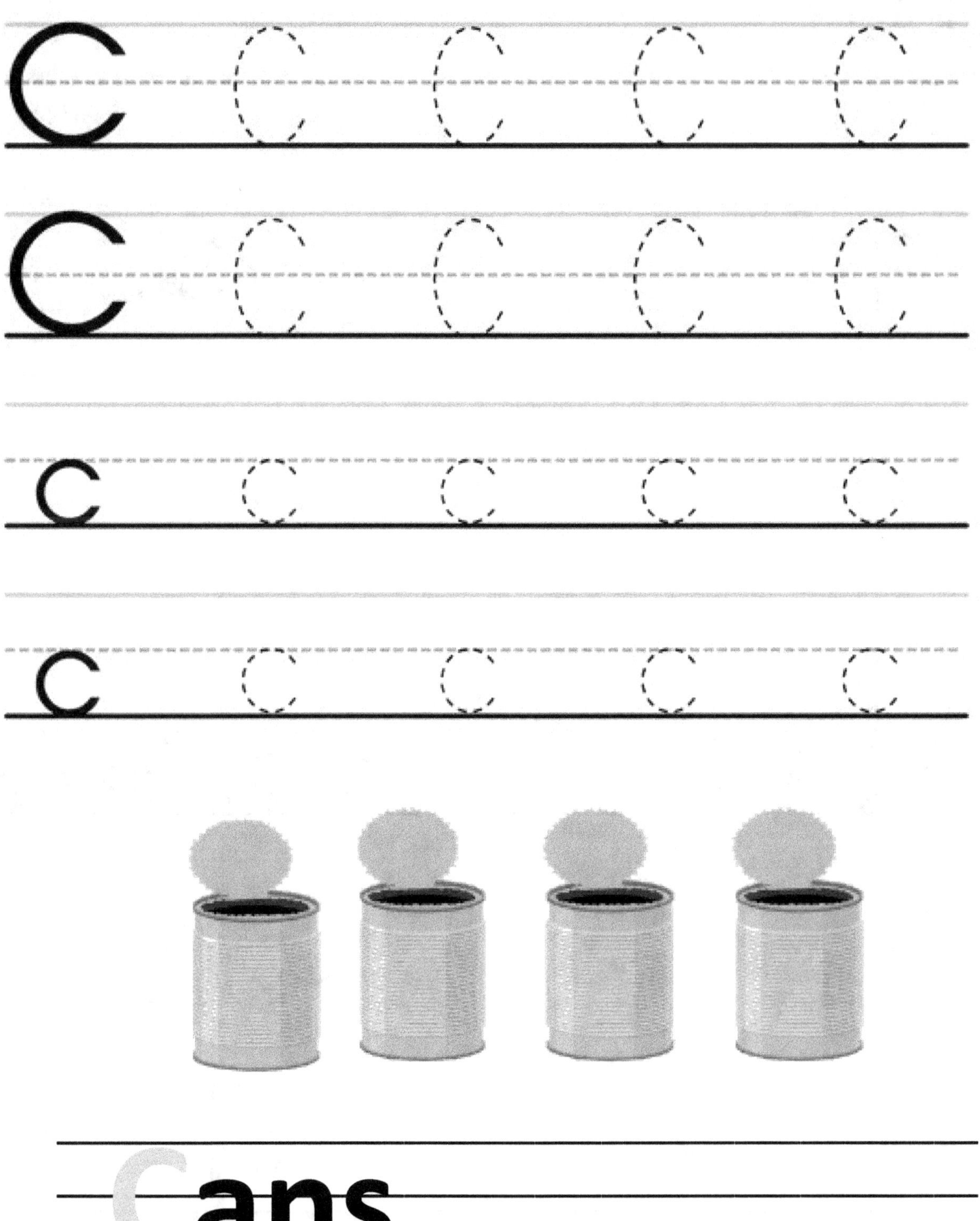

Cans

Cc

Cat coffee

Chair carrot

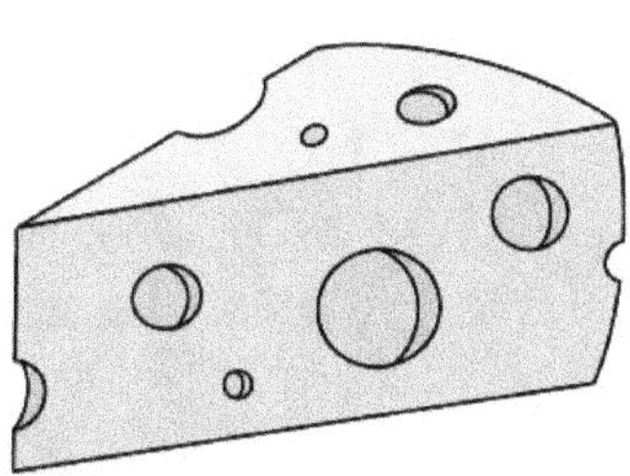

Cheese cake

Learn to write

Dd

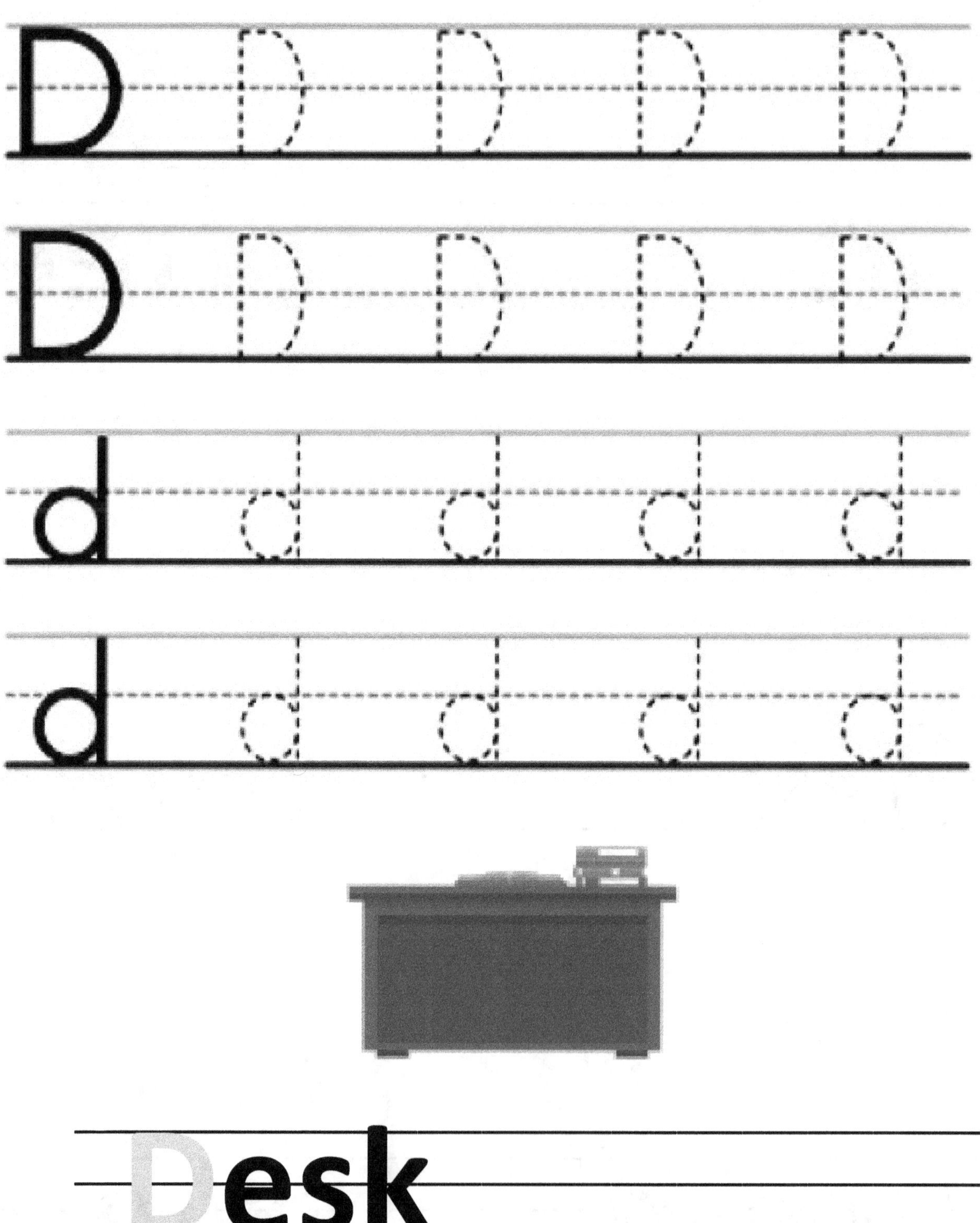

Desk

Dd

Deer dog

Donkey duck

Dad doll

Learn to write

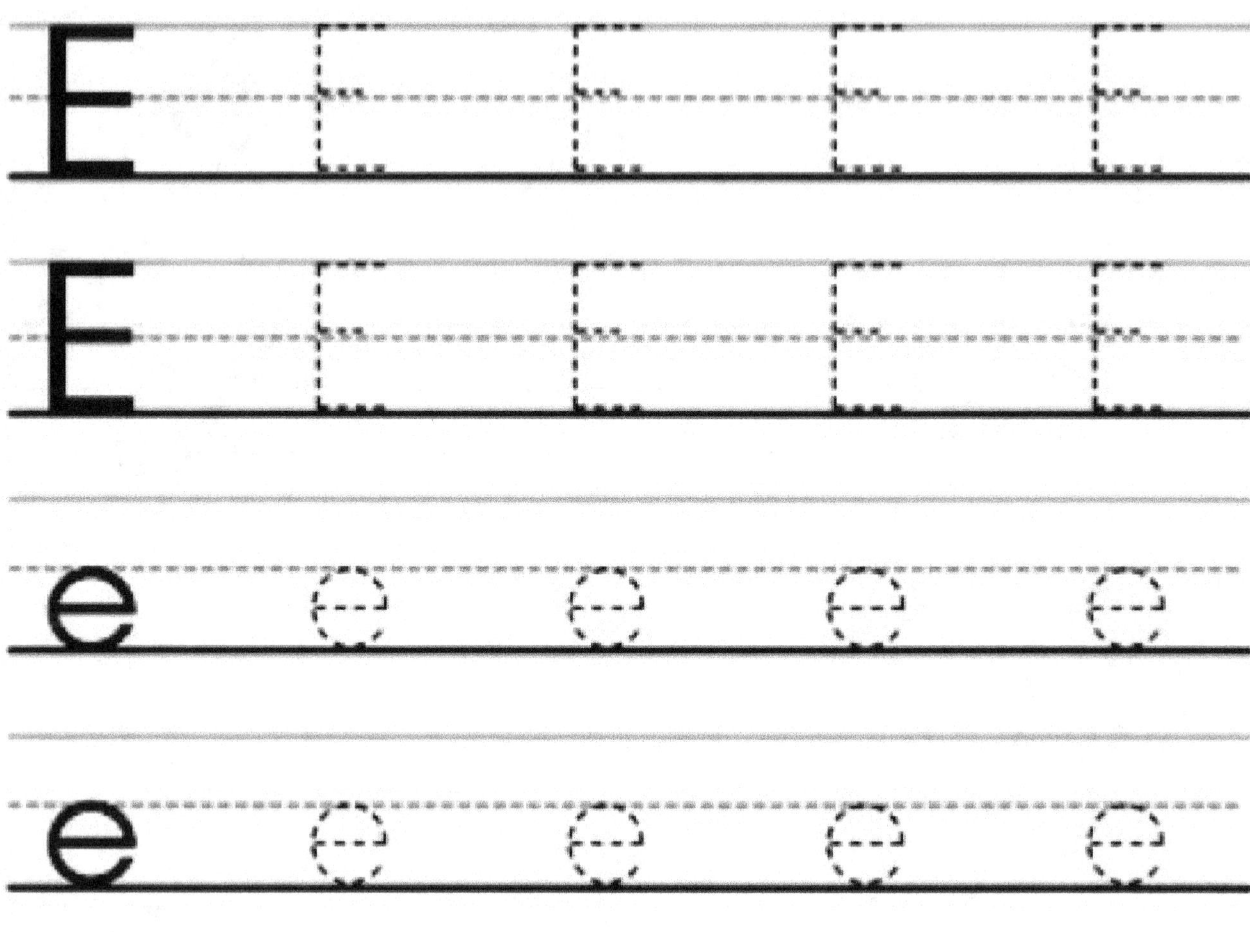

Elephant

Ee

Elk egg

Eagle ear

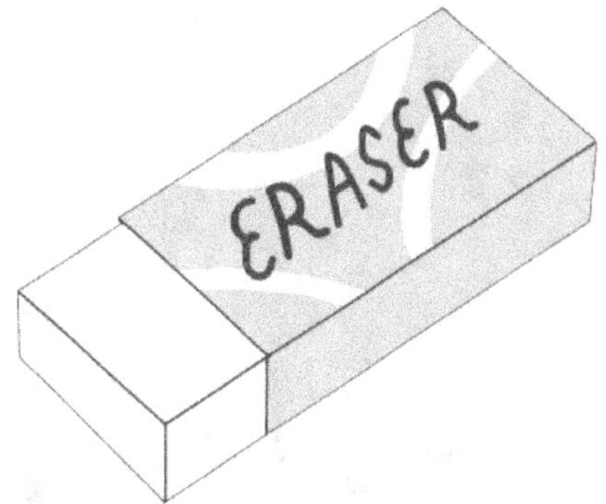

Earl eraser

Learn to write

Ff

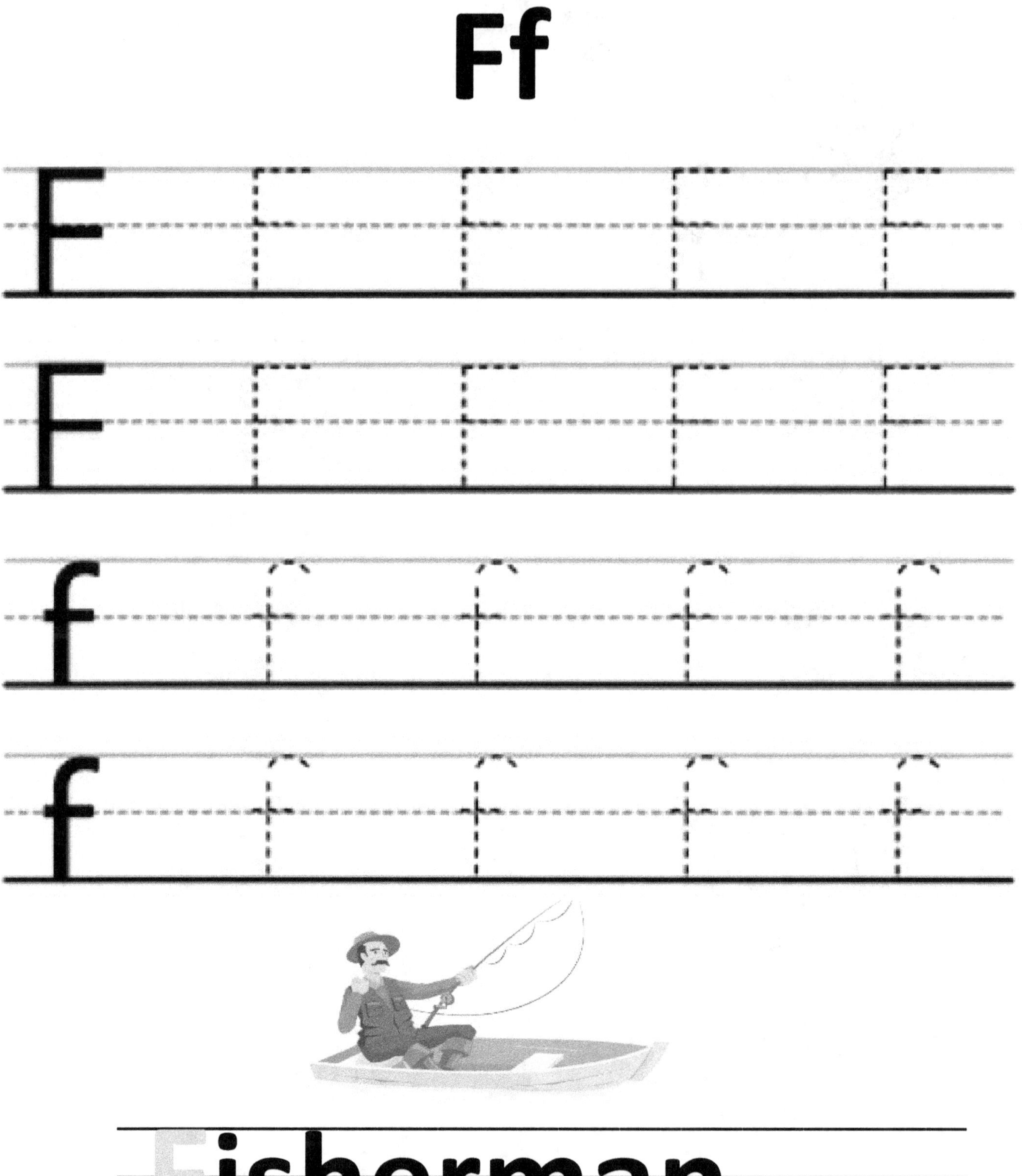

Fisherman

Ff

Fox

frog

Fridge

fan

Fish

flowers

Learn to write

Gg Gg

G G G G G

G G G G G

g g g g g

g g g g g

Guava

Gg

Goat grape

Gift globe

Gorilla glue

Learn to write

Hh Hh

H

H

h

h

Ham

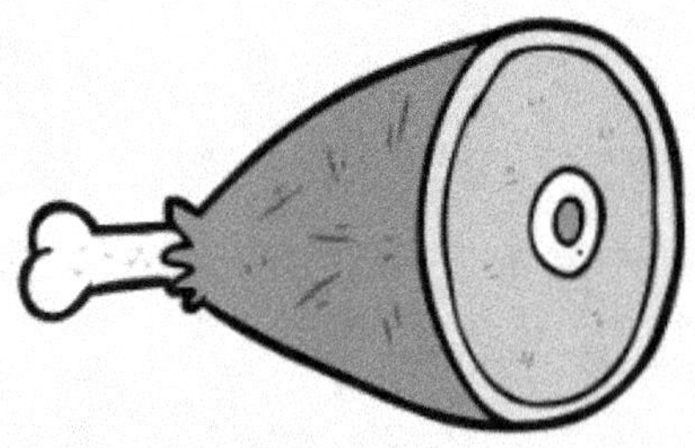

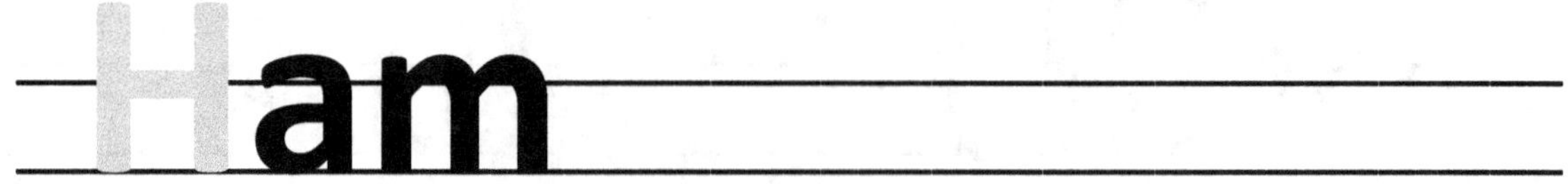

Hh

Horse hat

Hippo heart

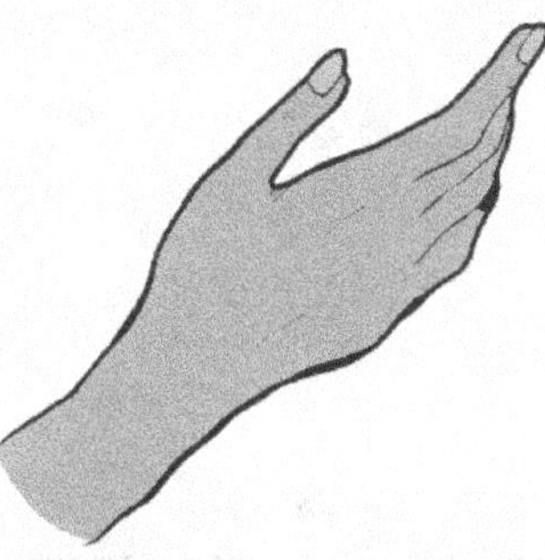

Hen hand

Learn to write

Insect

Ii

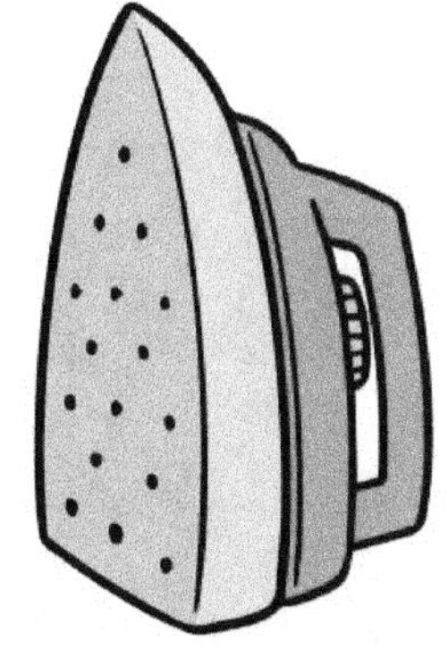

Ink

iron

Ice

igloo

Island

iguana

Learn to write

J J J J J

J J J J J

j j j j j

j j j j j

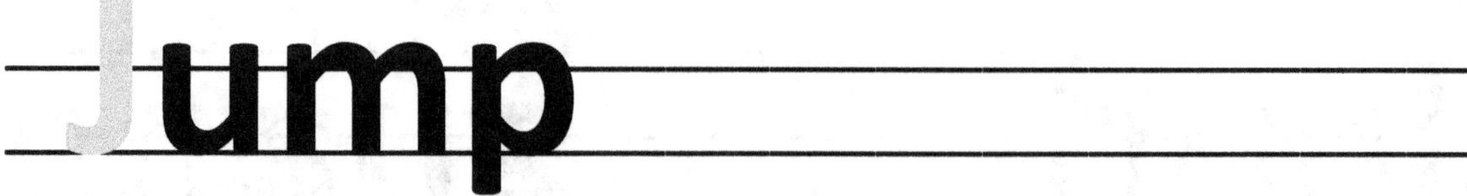

Jj

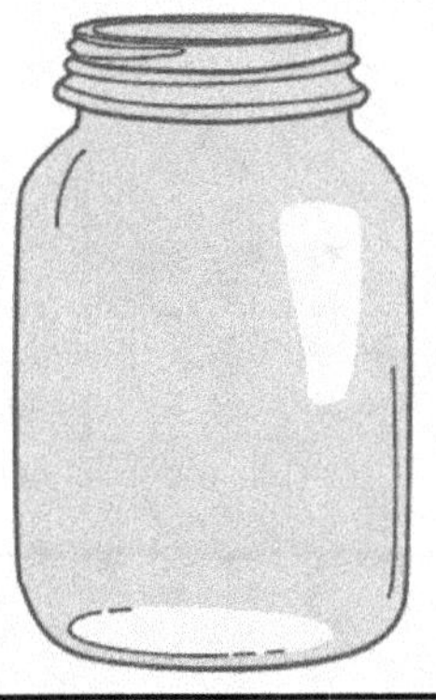

Jar

jam

Jelly

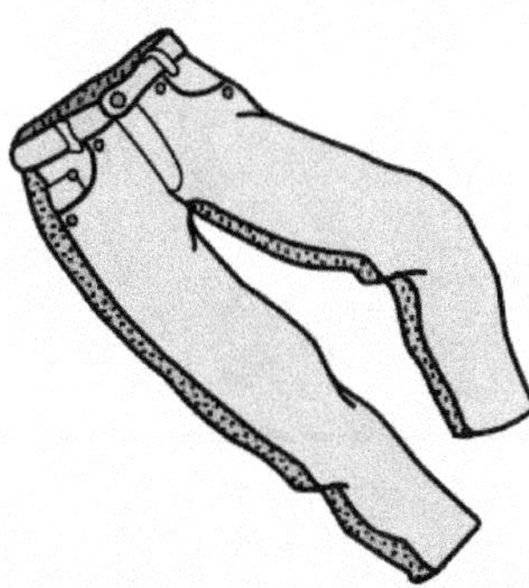

jean

Jacket

juice

Learn to write

Kk

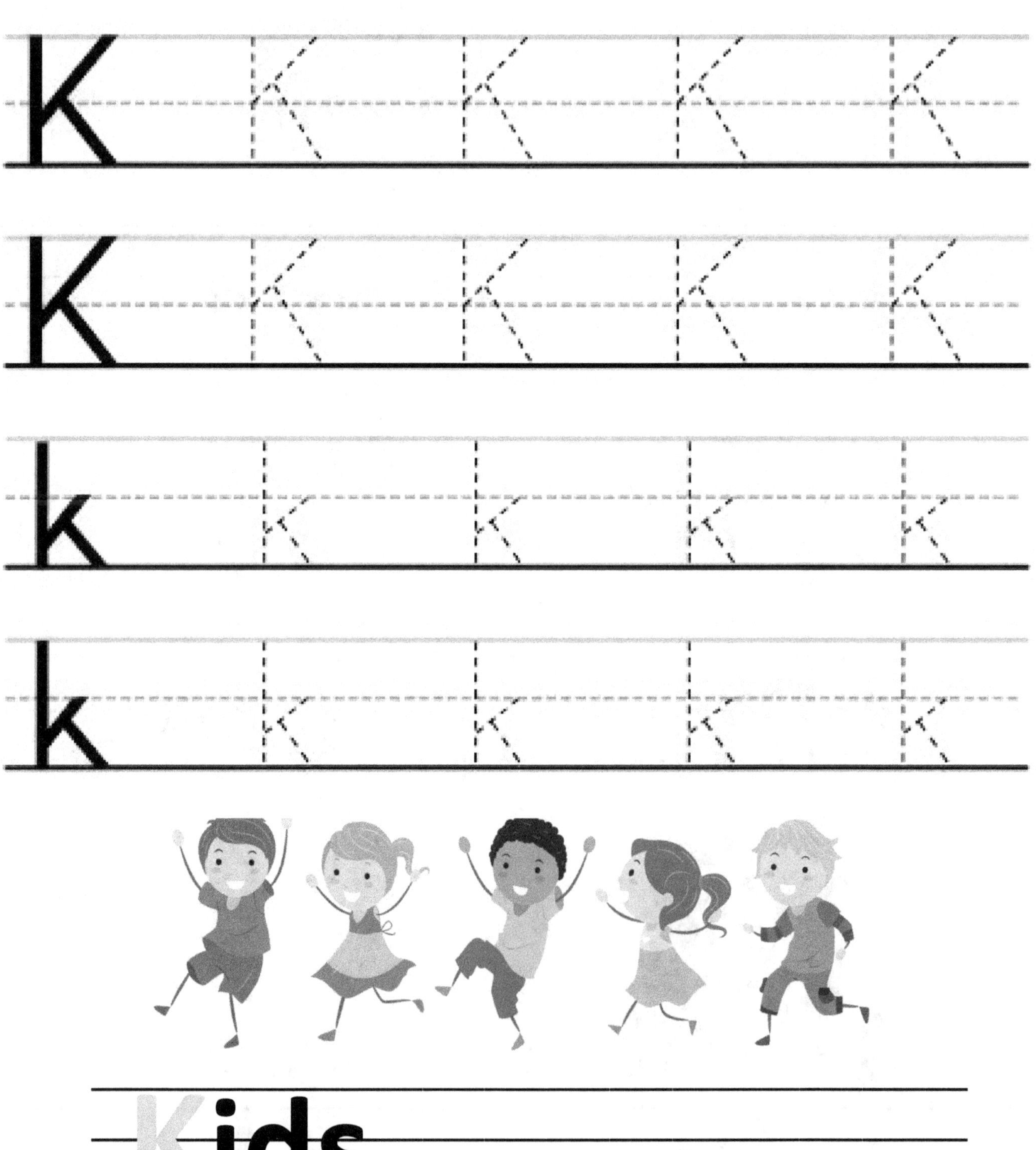

Kk

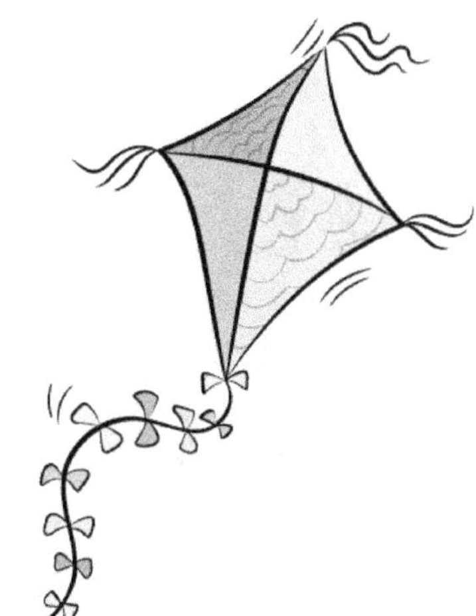

Key

kite

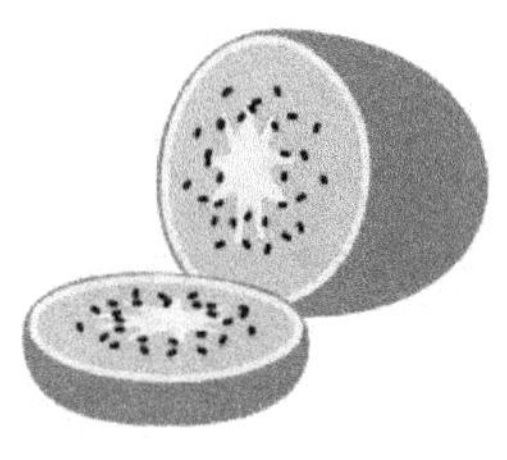

Kiwi

knife

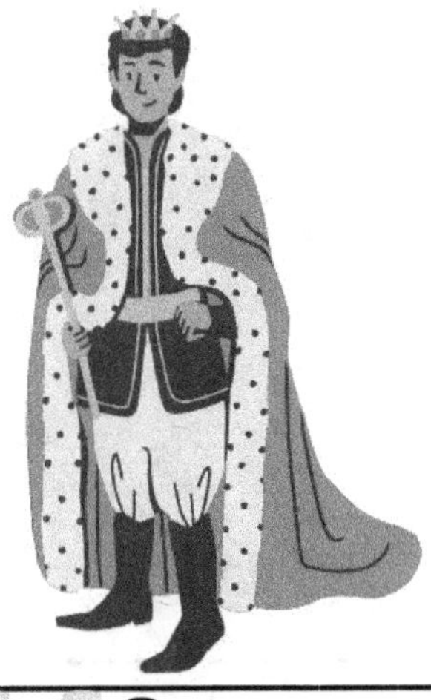

King

kitten

Learn to write

Ll

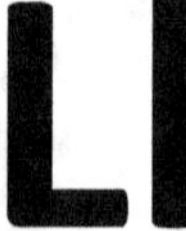

L

L

l

l

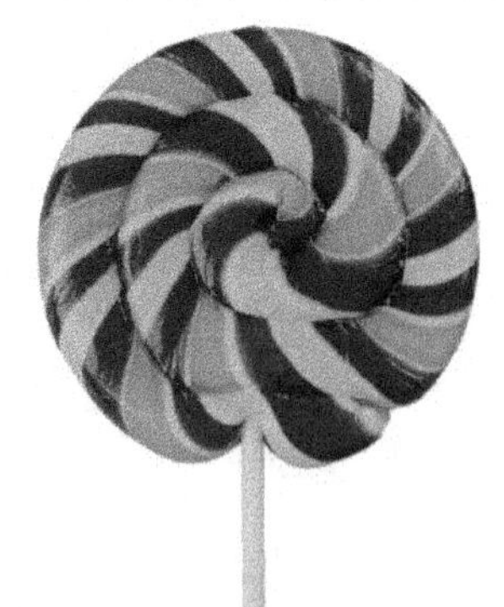

Lollipop

Ll

Lion　　log

Lotus　　lamp

Lock　　ladder

Learn to write

Mm

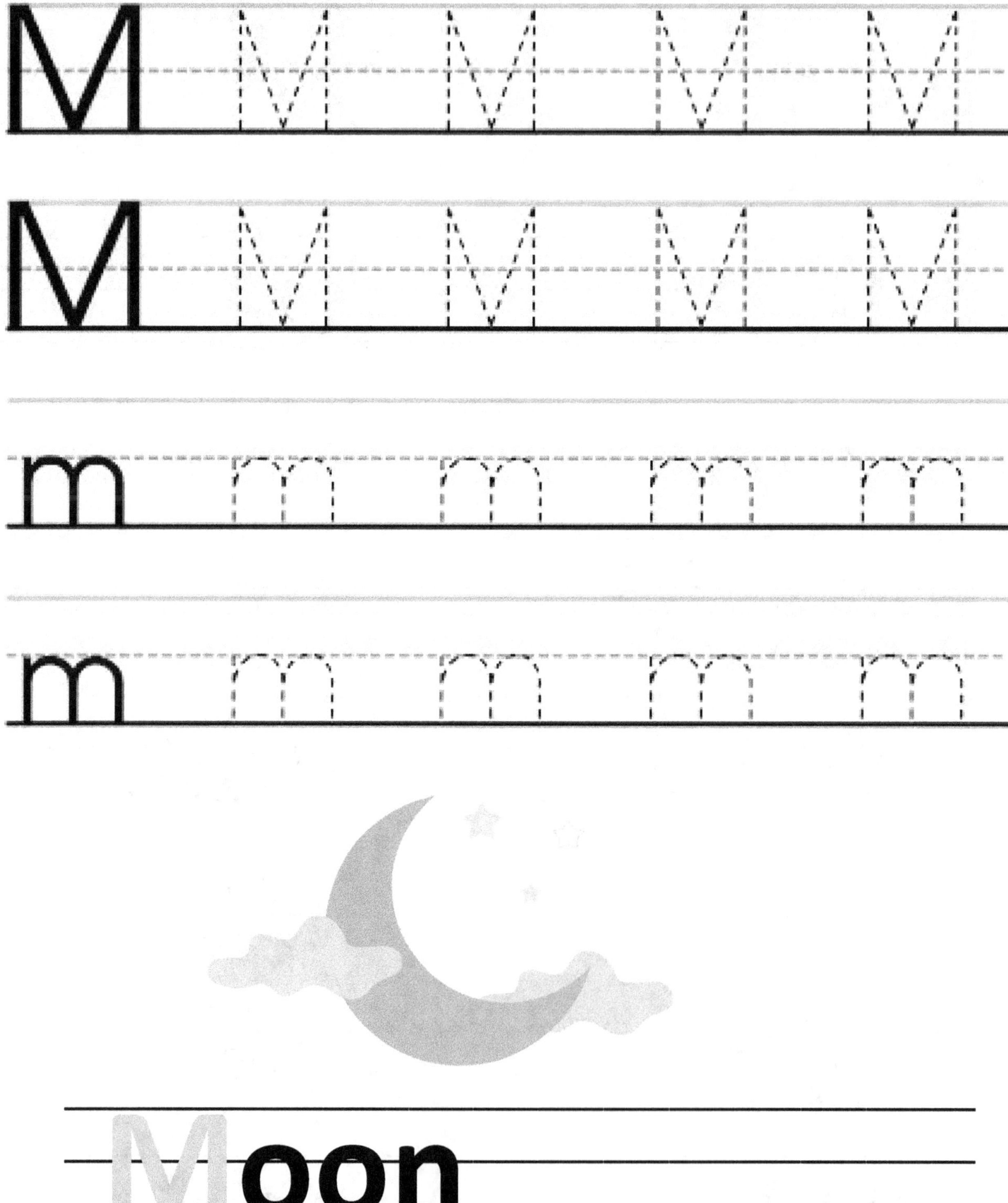

Moon

Mm

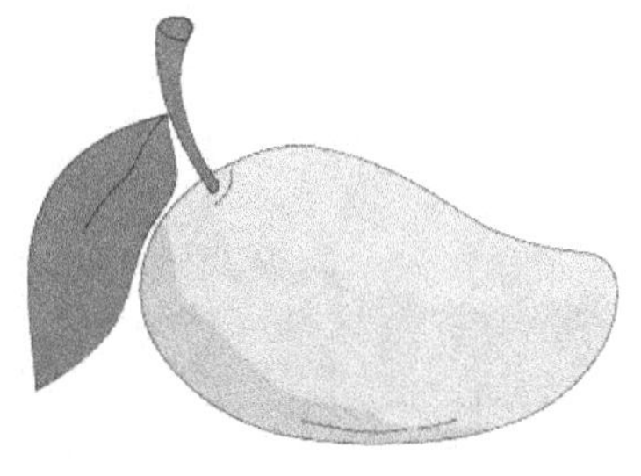

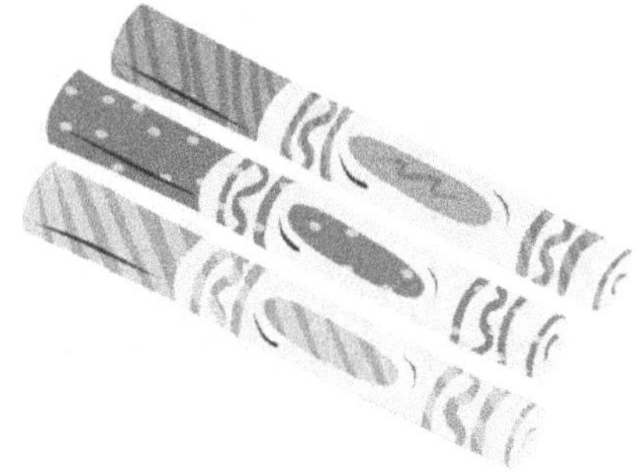

Mango marker

Mug mobile

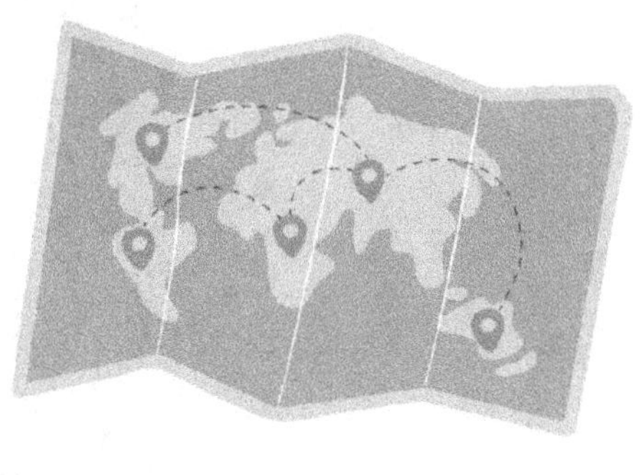

Mice map

Learn to write

Nn

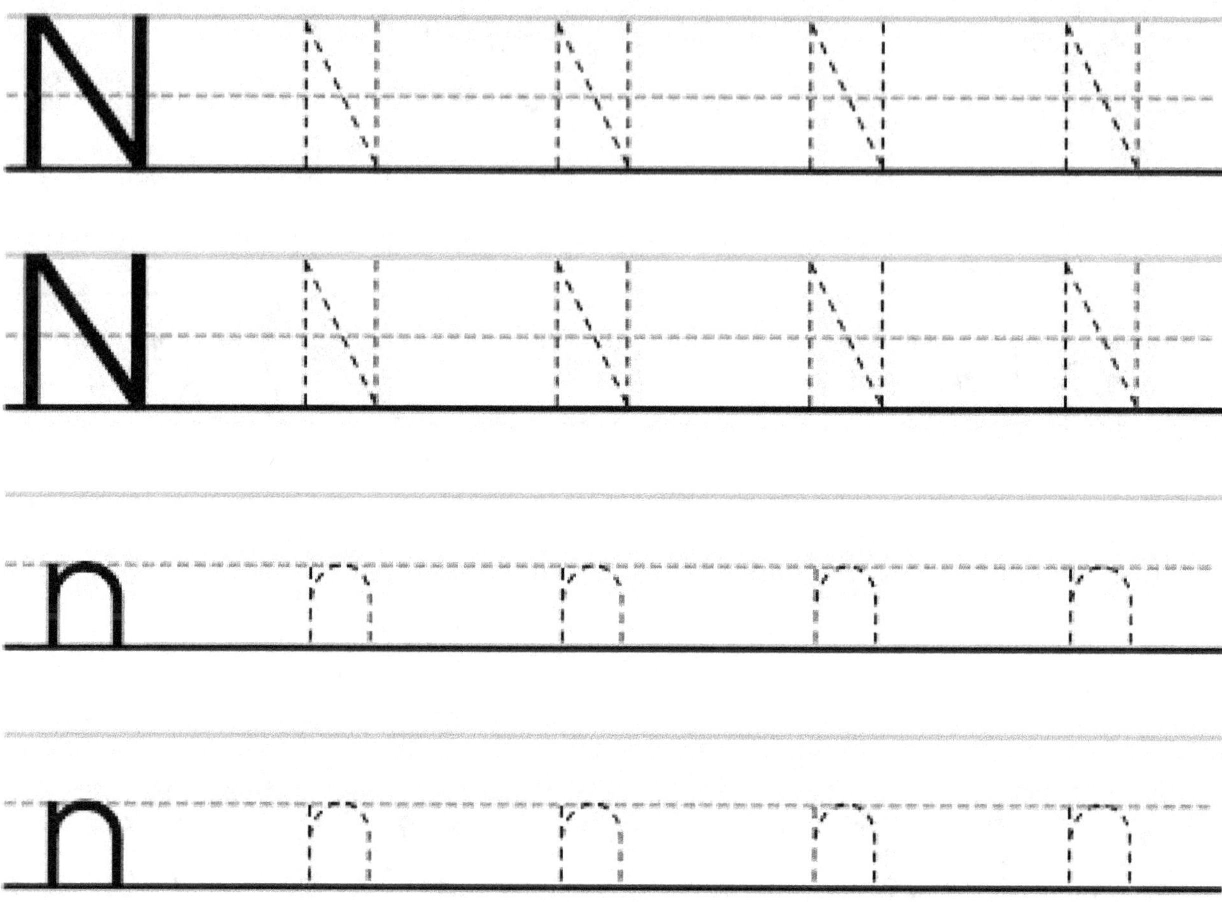

Nurse

Nn

Nest net

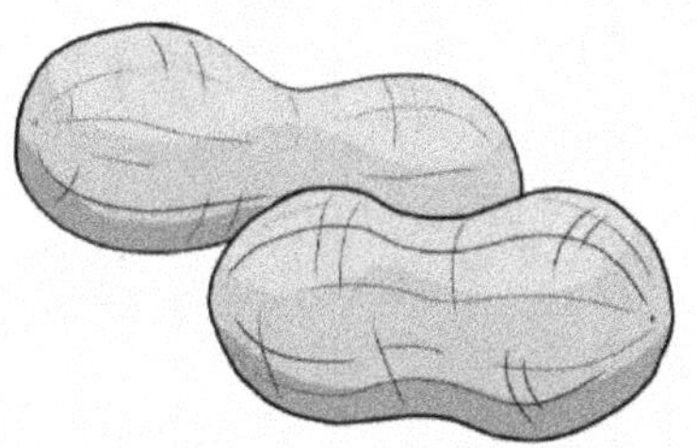

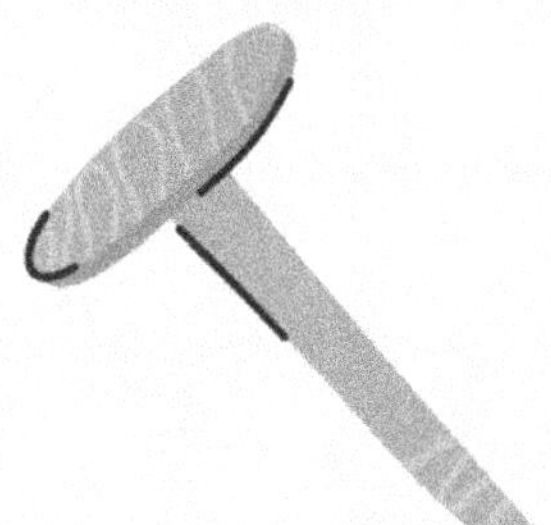

Nut nail

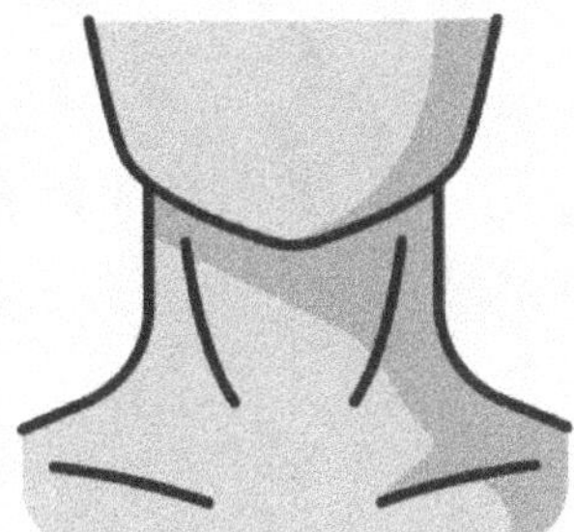

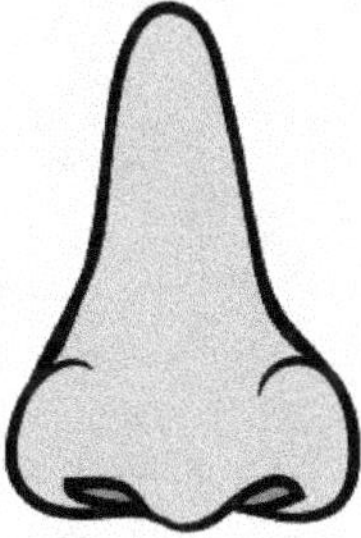

Neck nose

Learn to write

Ññ

Ññ Ññ Ññ Ññ

Ññ Ññ Ññ Ññ

Ññ Ññ Ññ Ññ

Ññ Ññ Ññ Ññ

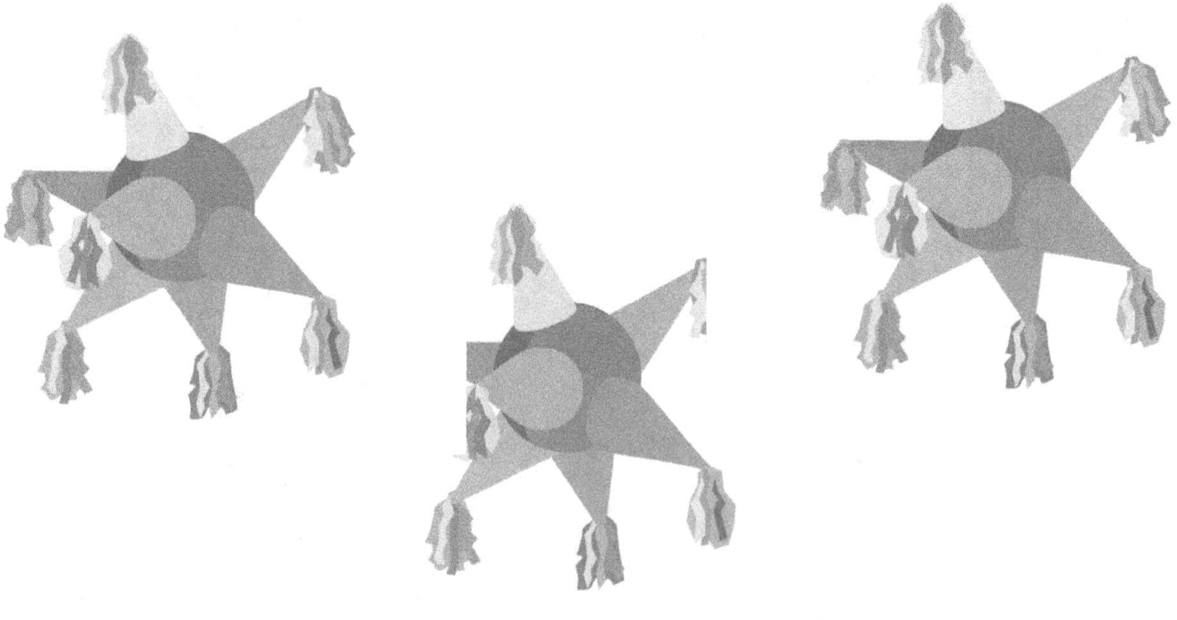

Piñata

Ññ

Niño

Señorita

NG ng

Bang sing

Ring swing

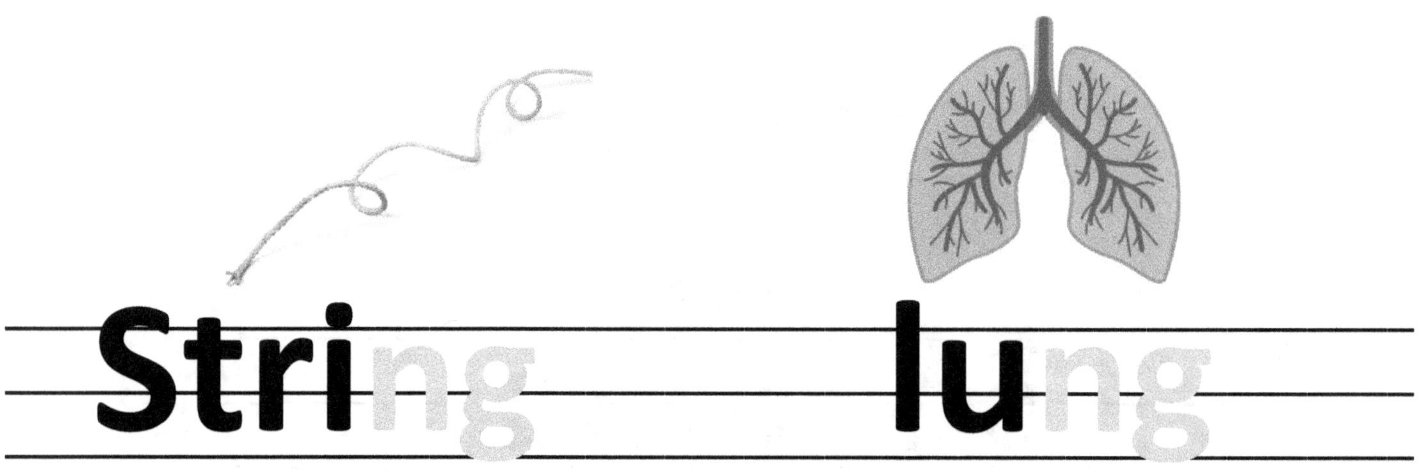

String lung

Learn to write

NG ng

Learn to write

Oo

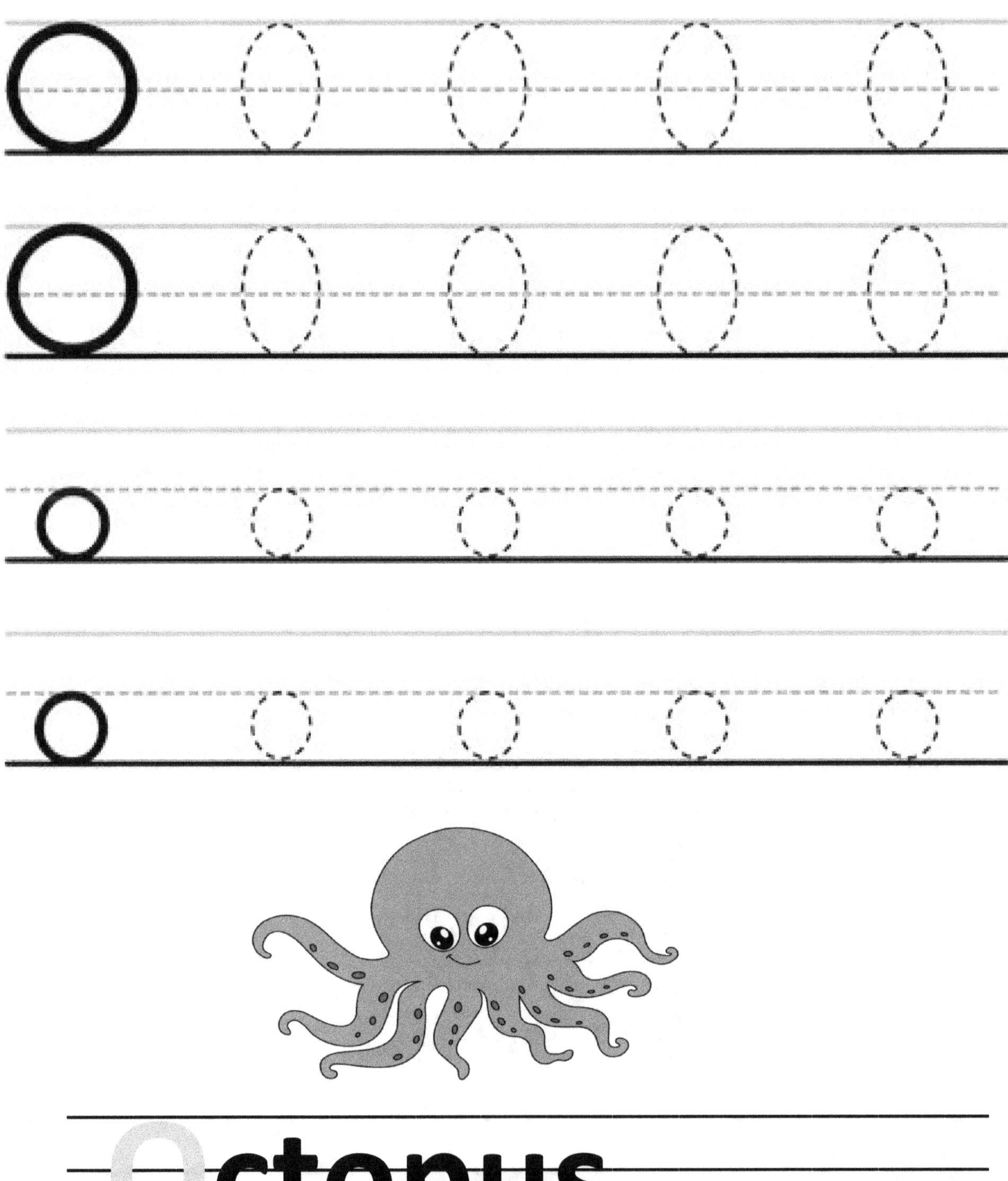

Oo

Orange onion

Oven oak

Owl ox

Learn to write

Pp

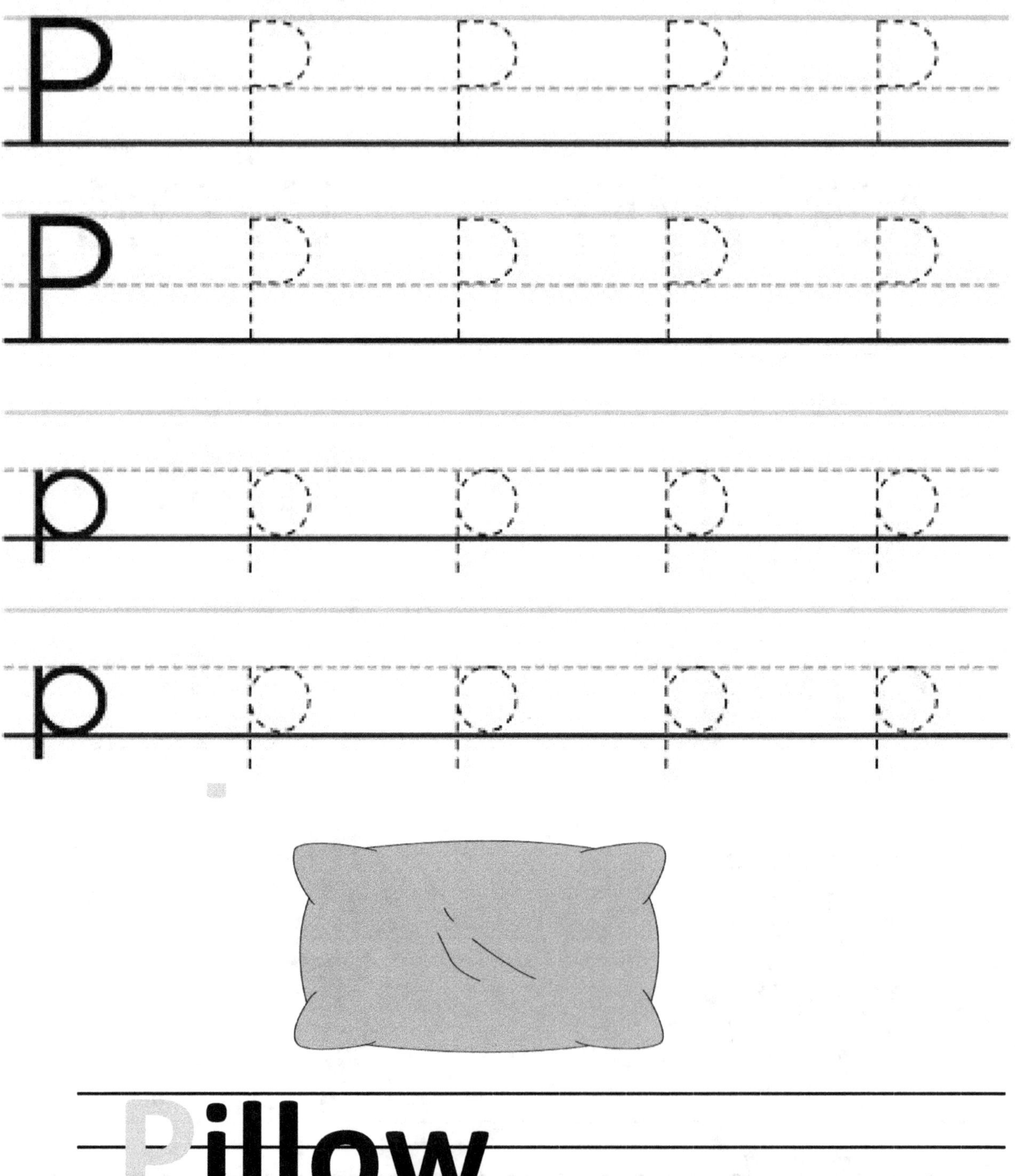

Pillow

Pp

Pan pancake

Pencil pineapple

Panther plant

Learn to write

Qq

Q

Q

q

q

Qq

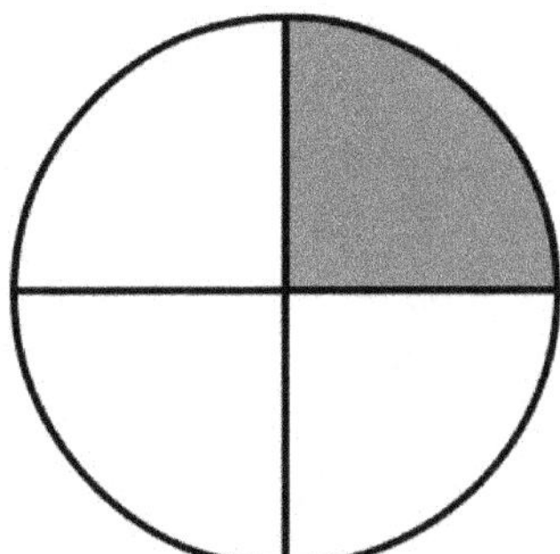

Question quarter

Quilt queen

Quail quiet

Learn to write

Rr

R R R R R

R R R R R

r r r r r

r r r r r

Radio

Rr

Rock racket

Rice rhino

Rose rabbit

Learn to write

Ss

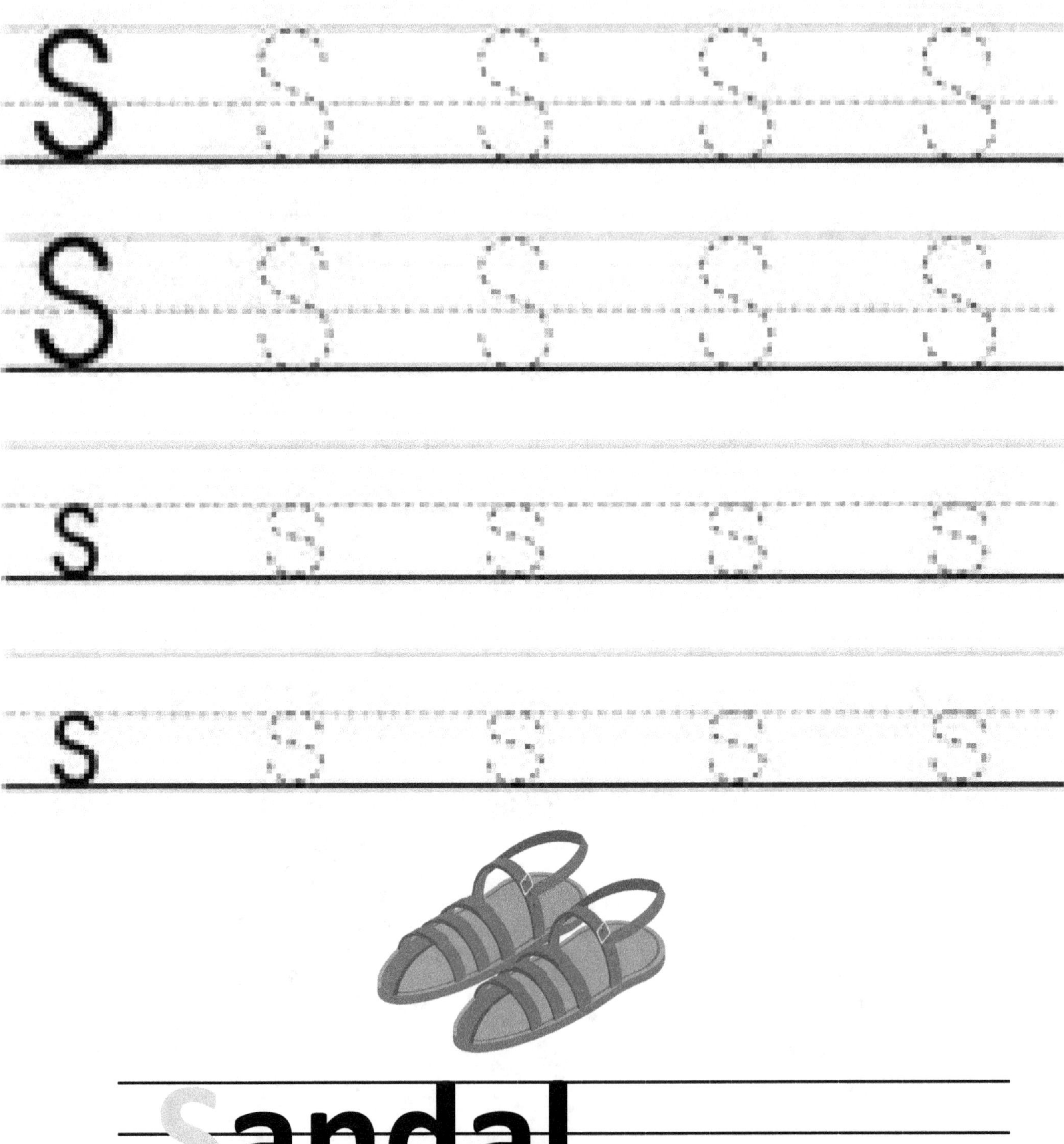

Sandal

Ss

Sun scissor

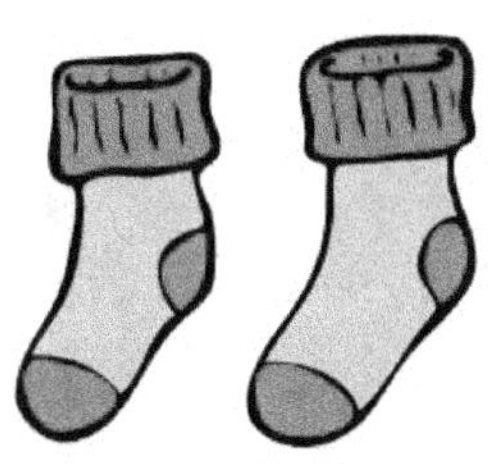

Socks shoes

Ship star

Learn to write

Tt

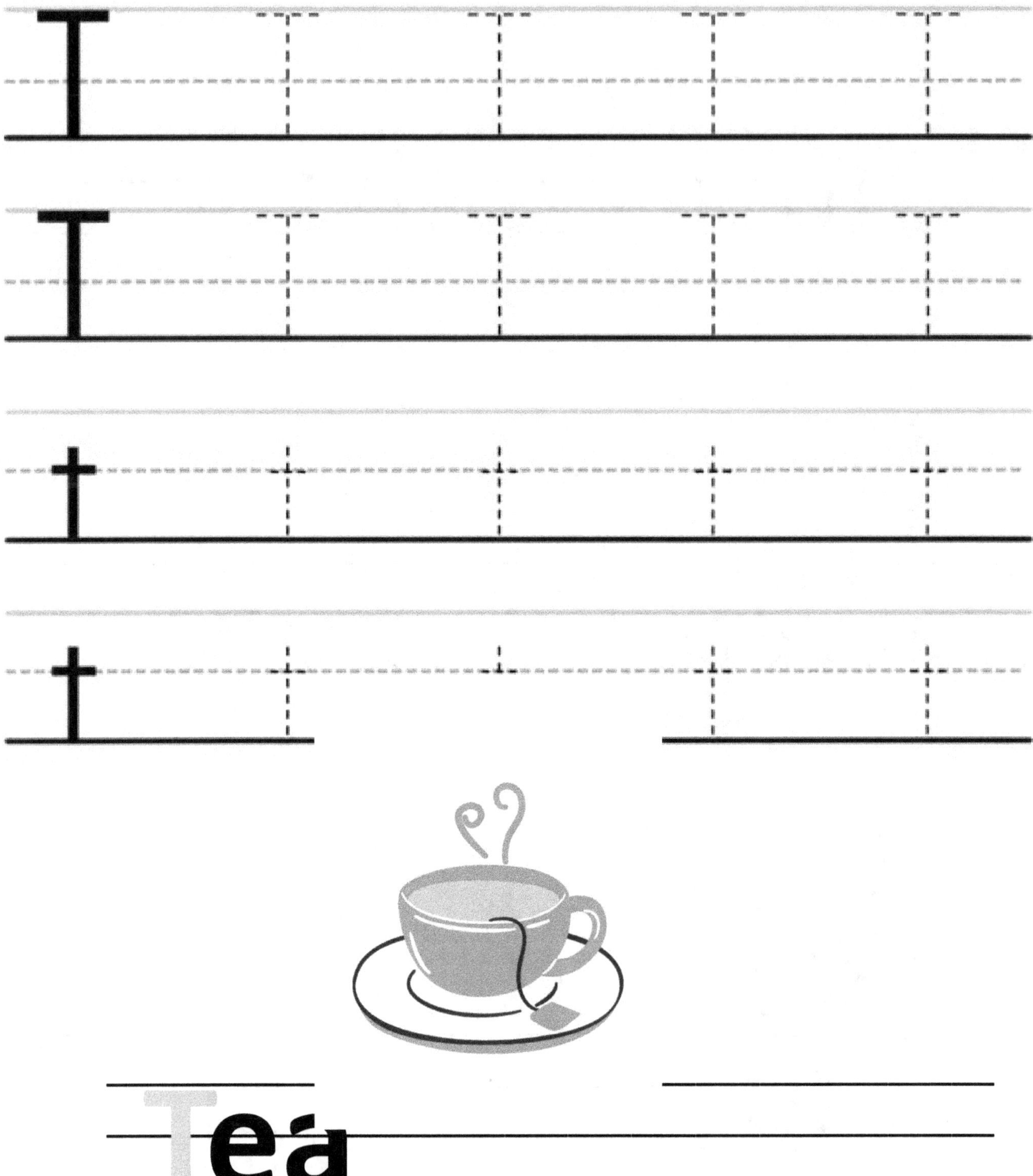

Tt

Turtle tree

Turkey truck

Tiger table

Learn to write

Uu

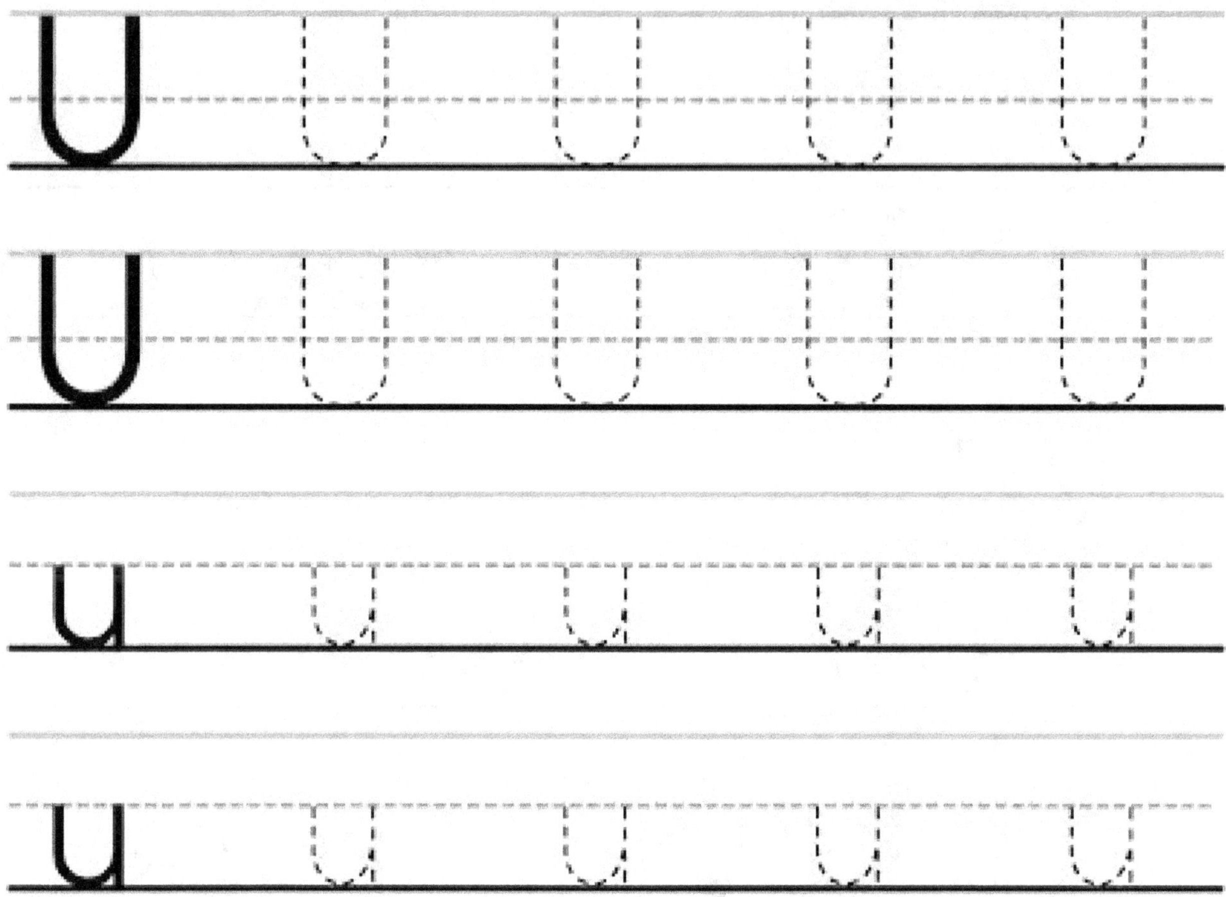

Uncle

Uu

Umbrella unicorn

Up ukelele

Uniform upset

Learn to write

Vv

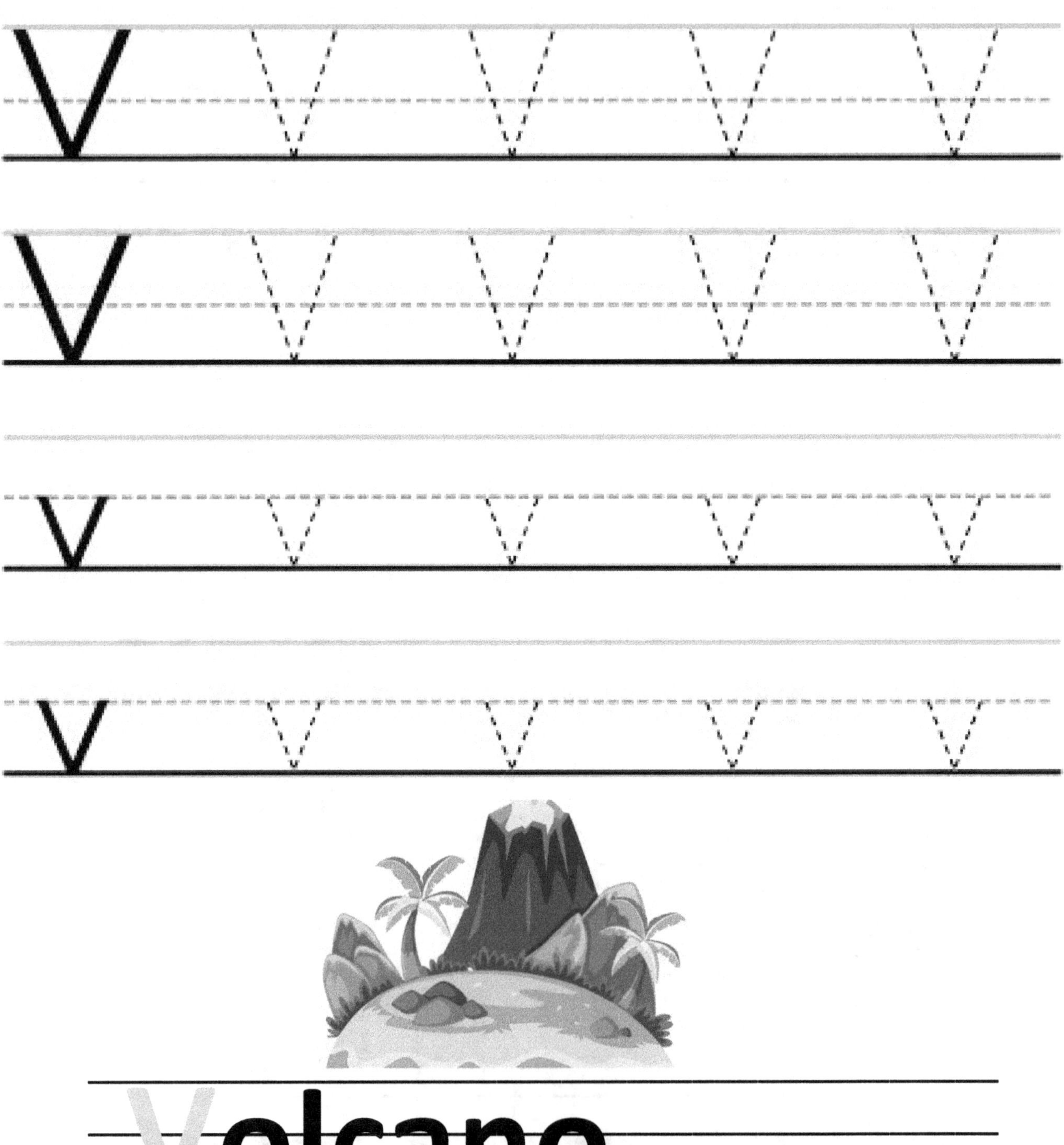

Vv

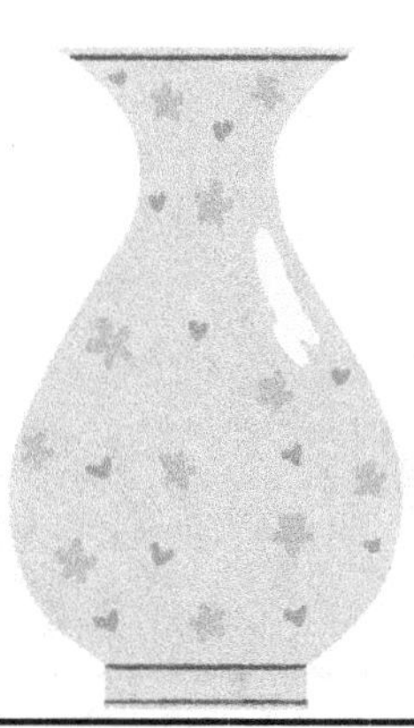

Van

vase

Violin

vest

Vine

vulture

Learn to write

Ww

Ww

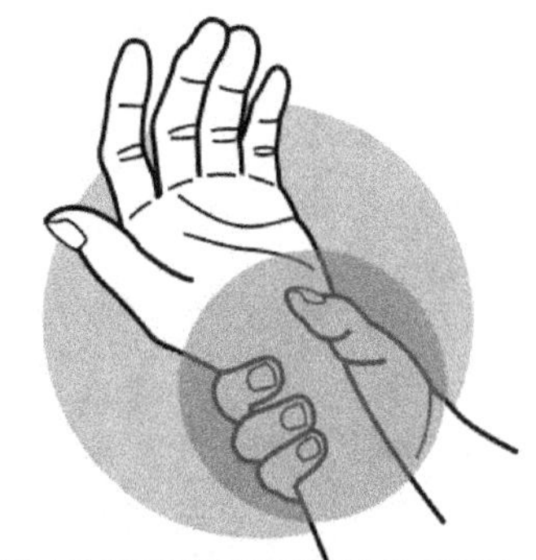

Wall wrist

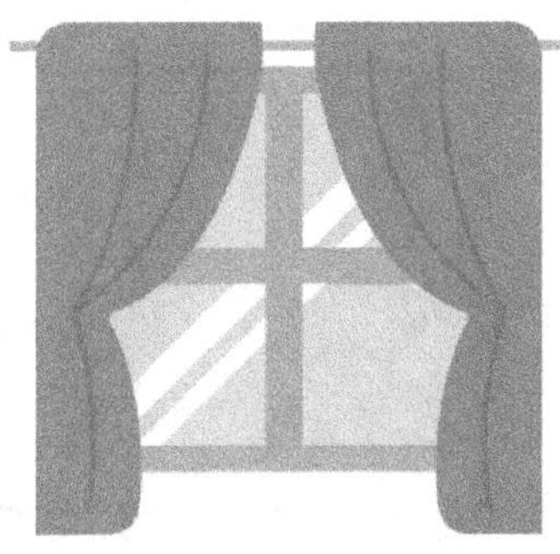

Window whale

Wolf web

Learn to write

Xx

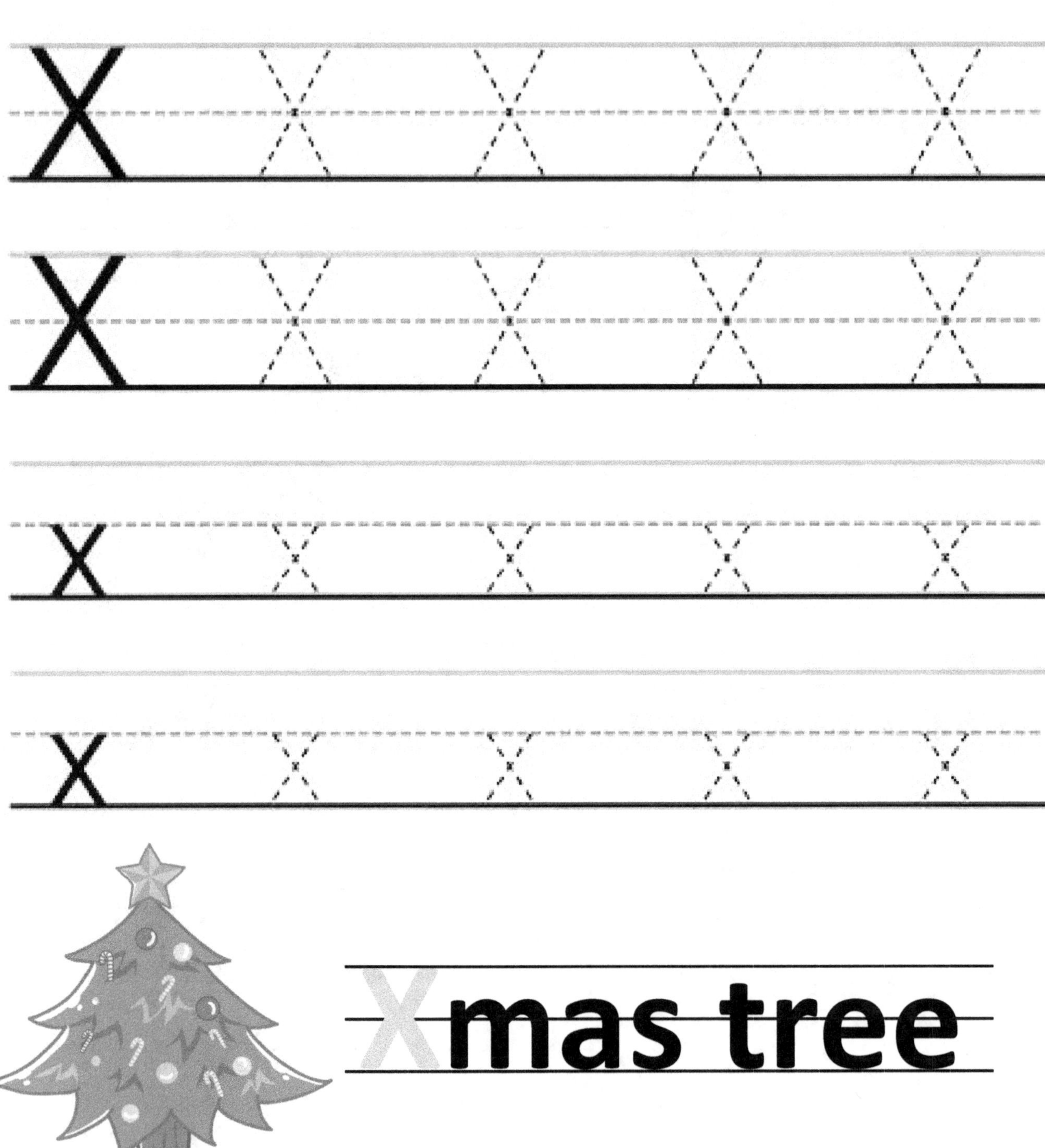

Xx

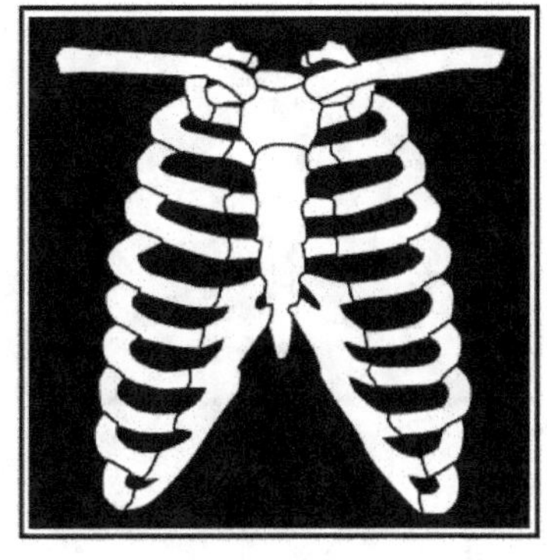

X-ray

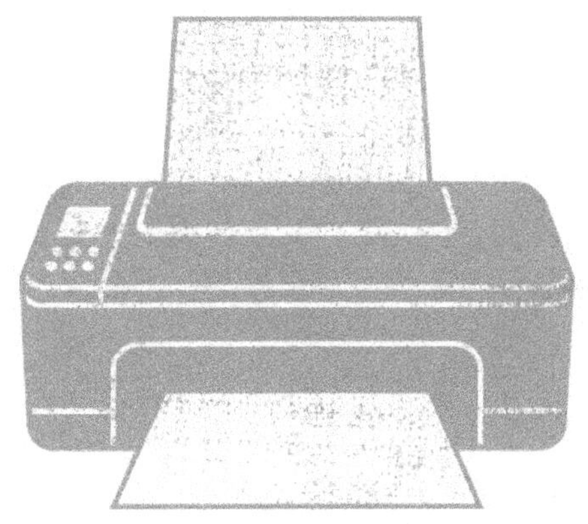

Xerox machine

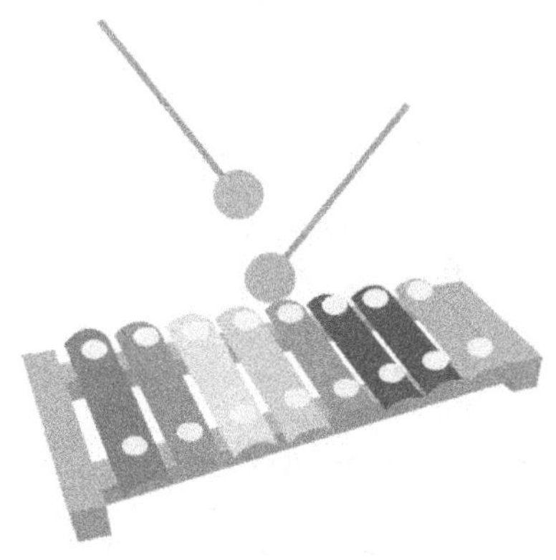

Xylophone

Learn to write

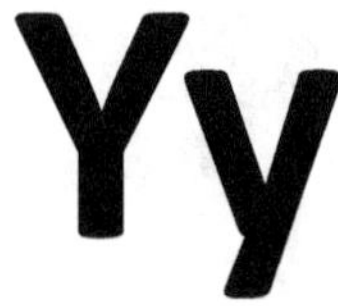

Y Y Y Y Y

Y Y Y Y Y

y y y y y

y y y y y

Yellow

Yy

Yak yam

Yoga yoyo

Yarn yolk

Learn to write

Zz

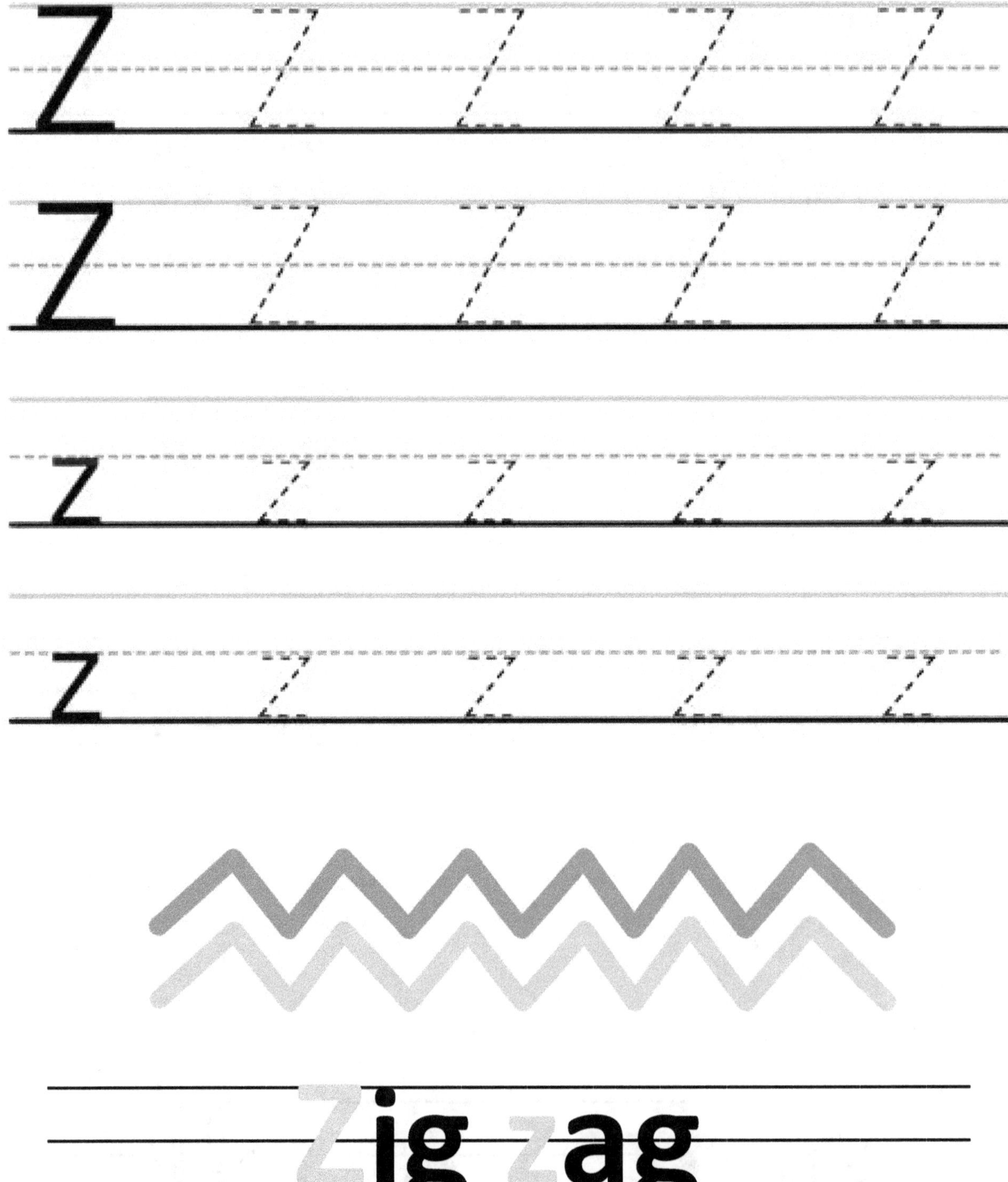

Zz

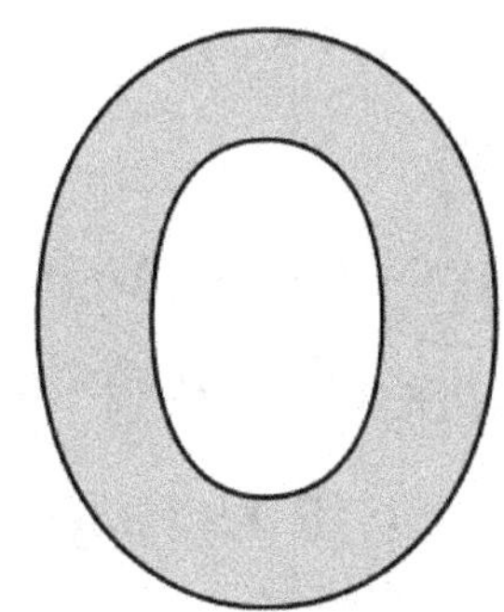

Zoo

zero

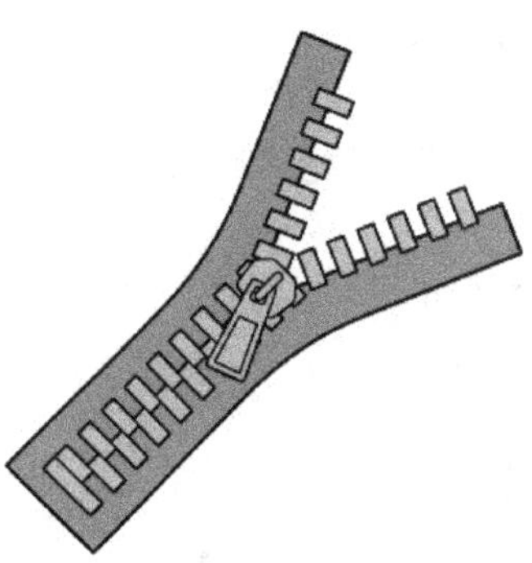

Zest

zipper

Zebra

COPYRIGHT © HAVE FUN WITH ALPHABETS
By ROY BASA

ISBN
Hardbound-978-621-470-342-5
Softbound/Paperback-978-621-470-343-2
MOBI/KINDLE-978-621-470-344-9

Published by:
Poetry Planet Book Publishing House
Rosario, Pozorrubio, Pangasinan, Philippines
Contact No.: 09554960044
Email: maritesritumalta@gmail.co

ROY B. BASA
LPT, PhD, DHum, DMin, DSc, FPOd, FRIEdr

Roy Basa was born and raised in Murcia, Negros Occidental, Philippines by Raul and Lilia Basa together with his other 6 siblings. He graduated his elementary education from Lopez Jaena Elementary School.
He then went to La Consolacion College, Murcia for his secondary education where he graduated as Class Valedictorian. He got his Bachelor's in Education major in General Science, Master's in School Administration and Supervision, and Doctor of Philosophy major in Educational Management at the University of Negros Occidental – Recoletos where he graduated with Outstanding Dissertation and High Academic Distinction Awards. He then took another masterate, the Master in Natural Science at the University of St. La Salle, Bacolod under a scholarship grant, Project – Free Paglaum.

He was a high school, college, and graduate school science teacher for 18 years in the Philippines and 3 years as a high school science teacher in Arizona and New Mexico, USA, respectively.
He was awarded as one of the Most Outstanding Teachers of the Philippines in 2016 by the Metrobank Foundation, Philippines. Recently, he was also awarded by Asia – Pacific Luminare Awards as "Asia's Most Remarkable and Exceptional Science and CTE Educator of the Year 2022.

ROZEL JAENA BASA, MBA

Rozel Jaena Basa was born in Bacolod City and raised in Murcia, Negros Occidental, Philippines by Romeo and Razel Jaena together with her other 3 siblings. She graduated with her elementary education from Murcia Elementary School. She then went to La Consolacion College, Murcia for her secondary education. She got her Bachelor of Science in Information Management and Master's in Business Administration at the University of Negros Occidental – Recoletos

She was a former Manager at Golden Sun Finance Corporation, Bacolod City, Philippines for 16 years. Recently, she is one of the Educational Assistants for Pre – K to 2 at Shiwi Ts'ana Elementary School, Zuni, New Mexico, USA.

www.ingramcontent.com/pod-product-compliance
Lightning Source LLC
LaVergne TN
LVHW060416200726
843506LV00007B/462

* 9 7 8 6 2 1 4 7 0 3 4 4 9 *